©1998 Contemporary Applied Arts
and Telos Art Publishing

Published in Great Britain by Contemporary Applied Arts
2 Percy Street London W I P 9FA www.caa.org.uk
in association with Telos Art Publishing
PO Box 125 Winchester SO23 7UJ www.telos.net

Edited by Tanya Harrod and Mary La Trobe-Bateman
Co-ordinated by Sonia Collins, Gallery Administrator
Designed and typeset by Telos
Cover and title spread designed by Satpaul Bhamra
Printed by Steffprint, Keighley, West Yorkshire

ISBN 0 9526267 5 6

CONTEMPORARY

Photography credits
Edward Barber p50
Dee Conway p23
Bob Cramp pp49, 57
David Cripps Front cover, p35, pp79–80
Michael Harvey p77
LB&W p17, p83
Paul Louis p62
John McCarthy p27
Graham Murrell pp19–20, 29–34, 36–37, 39–47, 53–55,
59–61, 67, 74–75, 81
Oscar Paisley p3
David Parmiter p63
Charles Roff Back cover
Heini Schneebeli p65

Front cover
Mary Restieaux, Ikat Weave, 117cm x 73cm
Back cover
'Maker's Hands'
Previous page
Contemporary Applied Arts
2 Percy Street,
London W1, 1998

50 Years of Craft

APPLIED ARTS

Edited by Tanya Harrod
& Mary La Trobe-Bateman

Contents

Foreword

Reflecting upon half a century of creative activity, across such a broad range of disciplines as is the remit of Contemporary Applied Arts, cannot and should not be merely a retrospective activity. Tradition is not something that simply stretches back into time, but that projects forward into the future; evolution does not stop at significant anniversaries.

This book, then, rightly celebrates the achievements of fifty years: the achievements of individual makers who are leaders in their fields, and of a unique institution which has nurtured and supported them, while gathering and educating a public for their work. At the same time, not least because some of those individuals have contributed the essays which follow, it looks to the future. As makers reflect upon their own discipline and those others which have inspired them, they raise fascinating questions as to the directions in which the crafts are now going; as to how tradition and innovation are imperceptibly and inextricably linked. The works captured here and suspended in time are like stills, taken from a moving picture that is still running and that will continue to run.

The fiftieth anniversary of Contemporary Applied Arts is thus a moment for celebration, for congratulations to all those who have played their part, for admiration for the work and its makers, and above all for optimism. Of the strength of the tradition there can be no doubt; but of the innovative vigour and fruitful pursuit of new directions for the future these pages are ample proof.

Nicholas Mann
Director of the Warburg Institute
Chairman of the Council of Management
August 1998.

A Brief History in Time
Tanya Harrod

Craft Centre of Great Britain
Hay Hill, Mayfair, London, 1950s

British Craft Centre
Earlham Street, London WC2
early 1960s

The Crafts Centre of Great Britain, the British Crafts Centre and Contemporary Applied Arts – the names are confusing but all describe one venture which was born out of the exigencies of the Second World War. 1939-1945 was, surprisingly, a time of planning and consolidation within the craft community as a concerted attempt was made to ensure government support when peace came. In 1946 a council representing five societies – the Arts and Crafts Exhibition Society, the Red Rose Guild, the Society of Scribes and Illuminators, the Senefelder Club (devoted to lithography) and the Society of Wood Engravers – met to discuss a permanent London-based centre for the crafts. The wood engraver John Farleigh was the moving force and in 1948 the Crafts Centre of Great Britain was formed under his chairmanship, publishing a constitution and an impressive list of lay subscribers including manufacturers, publishers and City livery companies. That year the Centre was awarded a capital grant of £18,000 by the Board of Trade together with an annual grant with a ceiling of £3,000 to be matched pound for pound by the Centre. This was the first government recognition for the crafts, fought for by the crafts movement since the First World War.

The artist crafts have always been nervous about trade. The Arts and Crafts Movement defined itself against over-enthusiastic, thoughtless consumerism. In 1913, when a lively breakaway grouping within the Arts and Crafts Exhibition Society suggested opening a shop, the idea was rejected with disdain by the most senior members of the Society's committee. Subsequently, the inter-war minutes of the two main craft exhibiting societies, the Arts and Crafts Exhibition Society and the Red Rose Guild, make depressing reading, dominated by endless attempts to define the crafts – against industry and against fine art and, often, against sensible retailing practice. Not surprisingly, therefore, the Crafts Centre began as a place where customers were restricted to ordering work rather than buying it on the spot. But by the early 1950s Sheila Pocock, just down from Oxford and the second Secretary to the Centre, was grappling with the problem of replenishing stock, attracting customers and getting coverage in newspapers and on BBC arts programmes. Thus a showroom and a meeting place for makers had also become a shop. But industrially produced goods were excluded which meant that the crafts could not be contextualised, as they were in other outlets like Primavera, by being displayed alongside good design.

From the start the Crafts Centre was burdened by its paymaster, the Board of Trade, who channelled funds via the Council of Industrial Design (CoID). The Board of Trade demanded that the Centre's constitution include the improvement of industrial design as one important goal. It was evidence of the fragile identity of the crafts. For the Board of Trade 'fine craftsmanship' could not be an end in itself. The battles over funding which dogged the Centre throughout the 1950s and 1960s flowed from this demand by government – despite the fact that the Centre was doing useful things like administering a complex Purchase Tax remission scheme for makers and staging a rapidly changing series of mixed exhibitions. It seems paradoxical that just at the moment when large numbers of men and women were turning to the crafts, its intrinsic value was not recognised. A less critical friend to the Centre was the Duke of Edinburgh, who accepted its Presidency in 1953 and was an assiduous attender of exhibitions, regularly photographed robustly quizzing makers on their work and ready with well prepared speeches on the continuing relevance of handwork.

In the 1950s the Centre's funding made expansion impossible. As Sheila Pocock recalled, the Centre had some very distinguished lay members but 'I got the impression that the Establishment was quite happy about us but saw no reason to do much to help.' In 1957 a broadening of the Centre's remit was discussed, going beyond the focus on 'Designer Craftsmen in the Fine Arts' outlined in the Centre's constitution. The furniture designer, wood turner and Royal College of Art tutor David Pye, a fierce critic of the Centre, read a paper recommending the inclusion of anyone 'who makes something and makes it superlatively well', thus opening the door to trade craftsmen such as the gunmakers, cutlers and toolmakers whom he so admired.

Greater co-operation with architects, in effect a return to the roots of the Arts and Crafts Movement was also discussed. In 1960 a joint Royal Institute of British Architects and Crafts Centre exhibition, *The Creative Craftsman,* made the case for collaboration. However, *Crafts Review,* a lively journal run by the potter Murray Fieldhouse and much given to attacking the CoID and the Crafts Centre, published a negative review of *The Creative Craftsman* which argued that while the ceramics were of a high order there was a good deal of 'emasculated nonsense' in the exhibition. Why nothing by Henry Moore or Barbara Hepworth? Why no stained glass by Geoffrey Clarke? Only the pots of Ruth Duckworth gave the reviewer 'some promise that the crafts really could deliver the goods in the form of beautiful objects to humanise our personal environment'.

If to *Crafts Review* the Centre was run by 'a cluster of old hens brooding proudly and eternally over an egg that will never hatch out', some of the

When the Crafts Centre came into being I was 23 years old and had, like many ex-servicemen, wanted to create an alternative world to that of industry and commerce; this was the vision that the Crafts Centre stood for in those early days. Central London had an almost Athenian atmosphere, and craftsmen, musicians, poets, playwrights, novelists, actors and film-makers congregated at the same venues. Later they dispersed into their specialised activities, but for a while the Craft Centre was one such venue that drew them together; this was in spite of the rather dusty and dowdy interior that in no way reflected the superlatively wholesome craftswork that it contained, of a quality unsurpassed since.

Murray Fieldhouse

Parking restrictions around the British Crafts Centre were notorious, and the wardens ranked amongst the most zealous in London. Finding a big shiny black car on those yellow lines outside was like gold for a small and determined lady traffic warden, and we all gazed through the glass doors as she shook her head at the chauffeur's explanation, licked her pencil, and walked to the front of the car to take down the number. Her expression at finding no number-plate, changing to shock as a laughing Prince Philip, our President, stepped onto the pavement, was neatly caught on camera and appeared as a half-page photo in the Express the following day.

Ann Sutton

younger members were determined to rethink its *raison d'être*. In 1961 a sub-committee led by the letterer David Kindersley, the potter Victor Margrie and Gordon Russell, the distinguished furniture designer and former Director of the CoID, worked on a strategy paper, *Image of a Crafts Centre*. It concluded that the Centre had the unenviable role of filling gaps left by the CoID, the Arts Council, the Rural Industries Bureau and the commercial galleries. A broader base was suggested, taking in rural crafts, engineering and pure design. Other key ideas included removing direct control from the five societies which made up the Centre, the publication of a magazine, the creation of a photographic index, the appointment of a salaried Director and a petition to government for a more generous grant and equivalent status to the CoID. And from 1961 the Centre's Exhibition Secretary Tarby Davenport actively sought out talented makers who were not showing at the Centre. These included heavyweights like Peter Collingwood, Hans Coper, Janet Leach and Lucie Rie. With Bernard and Janet Leach, Davenport planned the memorable exhibition of work by Shoji Hamada held in 1963. On the morning of the opening an eager queue of collectors snaked all the way up Hay Hill. But money problems disrupted these attempts to reshape and reinvigorate the Centre.

In December 1961 the Board of Trade decided not to renew the Centre's grant beyond 1962/3 because, it was argued, the Centre had failed in its enforced commitment to the improvement of industrial design. As so often before and since, the Establishment remembered that they had warm, nostalgic feelings about the handmade. On April 21 1962 Niall Macpherson, the Parliamentary Secretary to the Board of Trade, faced a barrage of hostile questions from Labour and Conservative MPs. This was followed on May 18 by an adjournment debate on the future of the Crafts Centre led by the Labour MP Julian Snow, well briefed by his constituent, the silk weaver Ursula Brock. But for Macpherson the crux of the matter was the Centre's active contribution to industrial design. This he assessed as miminal and the Centre's turnover was, in his view, economically negligible: 'In 1960-61, the Centre raised only £1,225 from subscriptions – a good deal less than is collected in the average village for local purposes'. This unkind remark caused John Farleigh to weep.

David Kindersley bitterly pointed out that 'the whole of Macpherson's statement sounds as if it may well have been written for him by the Council of Industrial Design' – and the role of the CoID in the affairs of the Centre was ambivalent to say the least. The Director of the CoID, Paul Reilly, appeared to

take a broad view and in this hour of crisis offered to create an area to display the crafts, putting forward estimates to the Board of Trade for a reconstituted Crafts Centre within the Design Centre as well as asking for funds for a trial craft exhibition. But what emerged from the CoID's discussions was a determination not to go, as Paul Reilly put it, 'down the arty-crafty road' but to recast the crafts as a handmaiden to design. In a confidential memo to the Board of Trade it was argued that 'the Crafts Centre, with its narrow attitudes and its exclusiveness based on fine craft societies with more than a hint of medieval guilds, has tended to widen the gulf between the majority of craftsmen and industry.'

As well as enemies without there were enemies within. From the start there had been disagreements amongst members, with the Bolton furniture maker Harry Norris from the Manchester-based Red Rose Guild putting the Luddite point of view passionately and in the bluntest possible terms. In 1963 Gordon Russell introduced Cyril Wood, a former BBC director and the first director of South West Arts to the beleaguered Centre. Opinions are still divided as to Wood's subsequent actions. In 1964 he formed a Crafts Council of Great Britain, intended as a beneficent fund-raising body; but by September of that year he had decided that the Crafts Centre was a lost cause and should be closed down. Craftsmen and women, led by David Kindersley, rallied but from 1964 until 1972 the craft world was bitterly divided between those loyal to the Centre and those taken with Wood's undoubtedly dashing style. In the end a puzzled Board of Trade gave both bodies a small grant.

Meanwhile the Centre acquired a new chairman, Graham Hughes, the art director at the Goldsmiths' Company. He proceeded to reinvent the crafts to his taste. He found new premises for the Centre, moving it to a warehouse in Covent Garden (before that area was 'discovered'). The Hay Hill lease was sold in 1966 and the Centre reopened with a dazzling party at Earlham Street on 11 April 1967. Hughes was keen on parties and excitement - and serious innovation. He gave Gerda Flockinger a one-woman show in 1968 and she filled it with astonishing new work. In 1969 Ann Sutton showed equally adventurous 'textile constructions'. In a press release Sutton asserted 'Where the machine can construct it has been used, for the sake of speed... No "mark-of-the-maker" plays a part.' In early 1969 Sam Herman showed experimental blown glass and Hughes responded to this new art form by setting up and financing The Glasshouse in a banana warehouse next door to the Centre.

Hughes ran the Centre with a council but it was smaller and quicker to make decisions. A change in the Centre's constitution in 1964 had limited the involvement of the five founding societies and Hughes was to remove their powers entirely. Some of the old ethical arguments ceased to be aired. A flyer for the Centre announced that 'the Centre welcomes machine-made work provided it is one person's conception.' Some cheap and cheerful objects crept in - what one maker privately described as 'Carnaby Street crafts'. David Wynne the sculptor showed and Donovan sang at the opening. Yehudi Menuhin got involved, and even served on the Council. Ossie Clark exhibited dresses. The batik artist Noel Dyrenforth painted psychedelic patterns on silk frocks. Hughes retailed robustly, setting up outlets in North America, Australia and Tokyo. He made links with corporate patrons and included the Centre's members in the 1969 touring show *Skill* organised with the backing of Goldsmiths' Company and the Institute of Directors.

In June 1970 the Conservatives won the General Election. The assumption in the craft world – that a Tory government meant less money for the arts – proved incorrect. On December 3 1970 Lord Eccles, the Paymaster General, told the House of Lords that he was taking charge of the crafts together with his other responsibilities for the Arts Council and associated arts bodies. On July 28 1971 Eccles announced the creation of a Crafts Advisory Committee (CAC) to the House of Lords which was 'to advise the Paymaster General on the needs of the artist craftsman and to promote ...a nation-wide interest and improvement in their products.' 'Artist craftsman' had been the hopeful, poetic job description employed by Bernard Leach in his *A Potter's Book*. Lord Eccles did not elaborate on the genesis of the term but it was obvious where his sympathies lay: 'My Lords, I think I may say that this is a very difficult definition; but clearly there are craftsmen whose work really equals that of any artist in what one might describe as the fine arts; there are others who are really very nearly industrial producers. Our intention is to go for quality first.'

The Crafts Centre now had a new paymaster in the form of the Crafts Advisory Committee, led by one of their own, Victor Margrie. The industrial problem vanished, to be replaced by new anxieties. Margrie moved to create peace in the war-torn craft world and the Crafts Centre of Great Britain was merged with the Crafts Council of Great Britain, emerging as a new body in 1972, the British Crafts Centre. But the 1970s were to prove a 'harrowing period' for the Centre – despite an involvement with the Crafts Advisory Committee's Index of selected makers and responsibility for a new shop

A letter has been sent to Mr FJC Cooper to explain that one of his child's spoons had been presented to Her Majesty the Queen on the occasion of her visit to the Centre, and the Chairman had asked in this letter whether Mr Cooper wished to give this spoon. He felt that as a point of etiquette, the craftsman should be given the opportunity to pay for it himself. Mr Cooper's reply explained that he felt such gifts should be paid for by the Centre. The Chairman then explained that he had received a second letter from Mr Cooper asking whether it would be advisable for him to go into a modified form of mass production with regard to this particular spoon, for the American market.
Minutes from the 46th Meeting of the Council, 1 September 1950

2 Percy Street, London W1
Building Work 1995

established in 1974 on a prime site in the Victoria and Albert Museum. Margrie's Committee frequently called the Centre to detailed account and by 1978 the then chairman Archie Brennan noted 'an atmosphere heavy with apprehension and insecurity'. Good exhibitions were put on, despite all the financial worries, beginning with Ann Sutton's witty series of *International Exhibitions of Miniature Textiles*, started in 1974 as an amused riposte to the increasingly sombre *Lausanne Biennale* dominated by massive, sculptural hangings. There followed all kinds of memorable shows – Elizabeth Fritsch in 1976, Ian Auld and Gillian Lowndes and David Pye in 1977. But 1978 saw crisis. The Crafts Advisory Committee grant increased to £80,000 for 1977/78, and the V&A shop was taken over by the Crafts Advisory Committee (which in turn renamed itself the Crafts Council in 1979).

In 1979 Lindsay Wilcox became chairman and under his wise guidance the Centre made a recovery. 1982 saw the pioneering and international *Jewellery Redefined* and in 1983 Tatjana Marsden became the new Director of the Centre. What the chairman described as her 'very strong visual taste and aesthetic judgement' transformed its fortunes. Marsden brought in a whole younger generation who had graduated from college in the late 1960s and early 1970s. They were the darlings of the Crafts Council but she offered them a special sort of acumen. She made the basement of Earlham Street a shop, and upstairs created a deliberately cerebral gallery. She did not neglect craft which in terms of the 1970s might have seemed traditional, but she also launched a series of adventurous solo shows mapped with handsome leaflets with acute texts by Alison Britton. Her taste, Central European and honed by the Royal College of Art and by working for David Mellor, was impeccable and confident. In the spirit of the 1980s links were made with business and in 1987 the Centre set up a Craft Commissioning Service in collaboration with Business in the Community. A corporate membership scheme followed in 1988. In 1987 the Centre changed its name to Contemporary Applied Arts – because the word craft had apparently become associated with the 'worthy, homespun and the (frankly) boring'. Things went so smoothly that Annual General meetings were tame affairs, sales figures increased and a new worry developed – was the CAA so successful that it jeopardised its charity status? In 1990 – after a series of triumphant shows for, *inter alia*, Gordon Baldwin, Stella Benjamin, Walter Keeler, Sara Radstone, Michael Rowe and Angus Suttie – Marsden departed, to join the auction houses, which as Director of Contemporary Applied Arts she had seen as such a threat to craft retailing.

It was clear that from now on the CAA would be shaped by its Director as much as by its members. It was still a co-operative craft venture but the taste of the Director had come to be of paramount importance. Tessa Peters took over as Director in 1990. Marsden's venture into corporate crafts had been a part of the confident optimism of the mid-1980s. But Peters' Directorship was undermined by a succession of economic set-backs, heralded by the Stock Market crash of 1987, the collapse in house prices in 1989 and the devastating losses experienced by Lloyds 'names' in 1992. By 1991 Contemporary Applied Arts was struggling again. Pressure was being exerted by an ever watchful Crafts Council to go 'commercial', to put the shop on the ground floor at Earlham Street and move the more challenging solo shows into the basement. In March 1992 the year ended with a loss of £154,000. Again, despite the problems there were memorable shows of work by makers like Gillian Lowndes, Thomas Eisl and Steven Newell. In June 1994 Tessa Peters resigned and the present Director Mary La Trobe-Bateman arrived the following September.

Retailing is a magic, complex process. Sales were to increase again under La Trobe-Bateman's leadership. In 1995 she negotiated the sale of the Earlham Street lease and found new premises in Percy Street, the heart of Fitzrovia – an area with a craft history. It was here that Ethel and Philip Mairet set up their high-minded New Handworkers Gallery in 1928. It lasted just over a year. Contemporary Applied Arts in Percy Street is a rather different story. The architects Allies & Morrison have designed a handsome interior financed by a lottery grant of £235,000, one of the shamefully few so far given to a craft project. Launched with an opening on 16 January 1996, Contemporary Applied Arts is once again a success, if not in the same way as it was under Tatjana Marsden's leadership. Solo shows, for instance, are no longer the norm. In 1997 a corporate friends scheme was launched – in the spirit of the 1980s. An education officer is being appointed: success and charitable status can be combined. In 1997 the Crafts Council's annual grant was withdrawn, signalling a farewell to the paymasters and an end to a complex, often painful relationship. At present Contemporary Applied Arts flourishes because of the atmosphere created by the Director and her highly trained staff. The place bubbles with enthusiasm and efficiency and also manages to operate as a successful business. Many exhibitors are young and gifted, and encouraged by 'focus' showcase exhibitions, are able to respond to the imaginative and pragmatic way in which the place is run.

The crafts are being reinvented all over again; and the essays which follow are a commentary on this process of reinvention in the context of seven exhibitions put on at Contemporary Applied Arts during this anniversary year.

Contemporary Applied Arts
2 Percy Street W1
Opening exhibition 1996
Hand to Hand

The Banqueting Table: The Aura of Software

John Houston & Rupert Williamson

Rupert Williamson
Banqueting Table (detail) 1998

Rupert Williamson
Banqueting Table with 50 Candelabra 1998
Laminated veneered maple top with stained legs
1.2m wide x 6m long

Candelabra by:

Jane Atfield
Raef Baldwin
Alex Brogden & Anna Dickinson
Amanda Bright
Anthony Bryant
Helen Carnac
Lucy Casson
David Colwell
Steven Follen
Marianne Forrest
Jo Green
David Gregson
Tom Hill
Andrew Holmes
Simone ten Hompel
Illingworth & Partridge
Cecil Jordan
Chris Knight
Richard La Trobe-Bateman
Alistair McCallum
Michael Marriott
James Marston
Malcolm Martin
Jim Partridge
Bill Phipps
Catherine Purves
Howard Raybould
Hans Stofer
Victor Stuart Graham
Lucian Taylor
Adele Tipler
Sam Wade
Lois Walpole

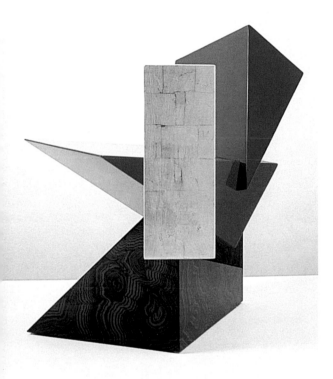

Fred Baier
Prism chair 1993
MDF, polyester lacquer
80cm x 45cm

right
Lucy Casson
Girl with Rat 1998
Recycled tin

Part 1: the Aura

Rupert Williamson's huge table, six metres long, is set ablaze with candles – with a table-top procession of glass and wood single sticks and branching candelabra by some thirty makers. A dozen dining chairs, each by a different maker, complete the scene.

All together, this array is a tableaux of propositions about the mysteries of making. Making as a unique phenomenon, faintly glowing with that twentieth century aura of authenticity which Walter Benjamin celebrated in the mid-1930s in his essay *The Work of Art in the Age of Mechanical Reproduction*. Benjamin noted that the existence of the work, 'with reference to its aura is never entirely separated from its ritual function. In other words, the unique value of the "authentic" work of art has its basis in ritual.' Attached to this passage is the famous footnote about the aura as a unique phenomenon of distance.

For all the domestic familiarity and the humanising function of these chairs around a candle-lit table, something of the sacred awe of the cult persists, and our perceptions are gladly distanced, and the aura briefly restored, even as we sit at the Banqueting Table.

For Benjamin, the prime model for the aura-less world was the flickering surface-less quality of film, dissolving older perceptions of time and space. But Williamson's table, as asymmetrical, polychrome, subtly skewed and referential as a complex totem-pole, has grown out of the screen and the computer program – not only generating his drawn ideas as rotatable 3D models, but precisely calculating every angle of every slow-turning intersection and penetration of surface. But such measurement does not diminish the space between the distant and the close. In this table and its companions the embodied dimensions and humane analogies of the made thing still assert that aura.

John Houston

left
David Colwell
C3 Stacking Chair *original design* 1983
Ash frame, oak seat
83cm x 46cm x 50cm

Part 2: the Software

My thoughts for the anniversary table were that it should express a new vision. I had just bought a computer and CAD software in the hope of generating simpler ways of producing my work, taken in by the buzz of the media exclaiming that the potential of the computer was limitless. The plan was to gradually master the software and make experiments. This tentative approach was soon abandoned when I learnt of the competition for the anniversary table. The opportunity to try and test out the potential of the machine was too tempting. The idea of developing ideas directly onto the computer, using the VDU rather than the sketch book, was one of those crazy thoughts one has in the bath. I wanted to see if the constraints of the computer would give my design thoughts new direction.

After a very short time, with my limited knowledge of the software, I was really struggling, spending many nights with my nose stuck to the screen and my finger on the mouse aching as though it was going to suffer a repetitive strain injury. The struggle I've had with my cantankerous machine and its software is enough to make a sane man throw the thing on the nearest rubbish tip. But for winning the commission for the anniversary table I might have given up in pure frustration.

Richard La Trobe-Bateman
Triangulated chair 1990
Ash, stainless steel cable
88cm x 54cm x 54cm

left
Ralph Ball
Chair for Changing Light Bulb 1997
Steel, maple, canvas
210cm x 40cm

right
Jane Atfield
RCP2 chairs 1993
Recycled plastic
55cm x 26cm x 30 cm & 81cm x 37cm x 44cm

In the end I was able to submit three proposals. They were an interesting mixture of concepts with complex arrangements of parts at odd angles, which I could only have developed with the aid of the computer. BC (before computer) I developed asymmetric forms using sketches and models. The problem with this approach is the difficulty of transferring the three-dimensional measurements onto a working drawing for making. The end product is very labour intensive and expensive.

One of the main restrictions to the competition was the cost, so if I was going to use asymmetric forms I had to find a way of overcoming the working drawing dilemma. Although one might spend hours generating drawings on a computer, there is the advantage of being able to plot dimensions to as many decimal points as one could imagine. The dream was to press the button and a little robot would come out of the back of the machine and effortlessly make the image you had created.
The reality is one gets eye strain trying to plot the lines to 0.1mm onto a material which would like to be used with 5mm tolerance. It soon becomes apparent that when working on the computer one has to keep in mind the materials and processes one wants to use. The machine only draws lines. The finishing details and quality in the end depend on the skill of human understanding of materials and processes.

Back in 1948, computers were just secret code-breaking machines. Even in 1974, when I was starting out on my career, they were no more than number crunchers helping big business with their accounts. Linking computers with Arts was just science fiction. I hope you like the table which has been such a struggle to bring into being.

Rupert Williamson

Clay: Changing Scenes
Alison Britton

Alison Britton
'Pot With Pleated Spout' 1997
50cm high

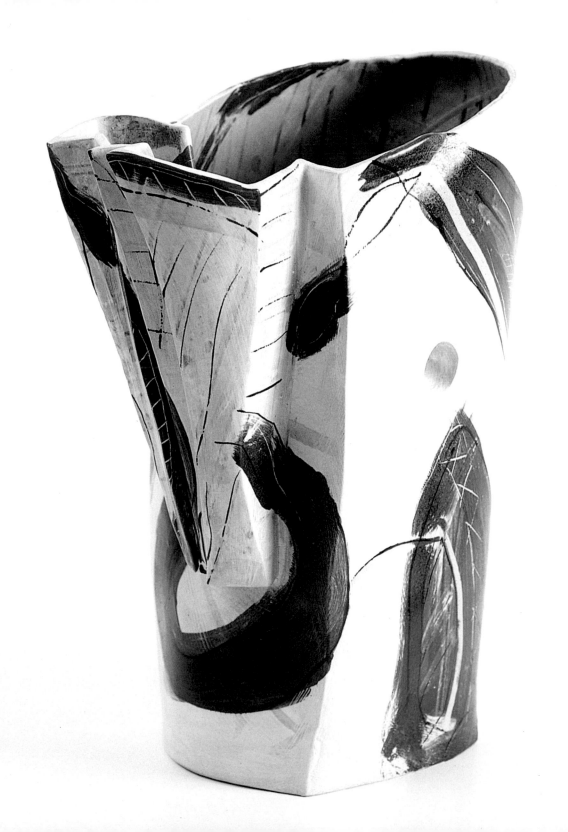

Gordon Baldwin
'White Vessel With Yellow Inside' 1997
38cm high

above on shelf
Gwyn Hanssen Pigott
'Two Jugs and a Bowl' 1997
'Grand Still Life' 1997

right
Gwyn Hanssen Pigott
'Grand Still Life' 1997
23cm high

The continuous survival of a membership association for 50 years is a remarkable phenomenon, especially where profits, egos, reputations and taste are involved. Under none of its titles, I suspect, has Contemporary Applied Arts been entirely without stresses and squabbles, periods of crisis and near financial ruin; and others of buoyant cutting-edge success. Britain must have enough good makers and a sufficiently responsive public for the ship, with its caring crew, to have steamed on somehow through all those years.

The British 'Craft Scene', as it has ebbed and flowed through the last century, has, firstly, much to do with our interesting desire to mix gentlemanly and artisan approaches, rooted in Ruskin and Morris; restated by Leach, and developed in art education. Besides being deeply conservative, the craft movement has kept alive an alternative philosophical and social position, sometimes Luddite, sometimes avant-garde, in response to the issues of the time.

A big interest for me is in when and why categories change, I realise; and where different species meet, the chances of overlap and hybridisation are great. This is why I have always been glad of venues like Contemporary Applied Arts, and the Crafts Council, that covered a whole range of media. I am intrigued by the way in which ideas seem to be in the air, across disciplines. What Michael Rowe was making in metal in 1977, for instance, was as exciting to me, formally, as anything happening in clay. So the mixed-media gallery is an ideal space, a place to share ideas.

But my job in this essay is to look at ceramics in the long record of exhibitions at Contemporary Applied Arts. It seems that innovation and tradition – the edges of the craft perspective – have both been covered. It is notable that the Leach Pottery, over forty years old by then, exhibited in 1964 and that in the same year a new wave of Ian Auld, Colin Pearson and Ruth Duckworth also showed ceramics.

When I was a student at the Central School of Art and Design in the late sixties I first went to the British Crafts Centre to see a Tony Hepburn exhibition. (Hepburn subsequently made his career in the USA). I hadn't known that such work existed in clay – sculptures like melting telephones, high-fired cast and collapsing forms with smooth dolomite glazes. My horizons widened. In 1973 the British Crafts Centre held the first exhibition of ceramics by Jacqui Poncelet and Glenys Barton, fresh out of the Royal College of Art. They made slip-cast bone china forms; geometrically precise forms in primary colours in Barton's case, delicately distorted bowls in Poncelet's. The Crafts Advisory Committee's flagship magazine *Crafts*, which began publication in March of that year, featured them in its second issue in an article entitled *Outside Tradition*. Its author was Fiona Adamczewski who then worked at the Centre. She describes Glenys Barton as 'very much a person of her time, tough, sensitive, highly intelligent, a little alarming and very impressive: "I dont really think I am a craftsman. Making things really bores me. I'm much more excited by the process of conceiving the idea." ' The publicity for the show featured a picture of them as striking, even glamorous, young women. The image of the crafts shifted a little.

below
William Newland
'Wiggly Waggly Dish' 1989
60cm x 70cm

left, foreground
Philip Eglin
Three Buckets
'Bucket' 1997 38cm high
'Hugh and Divine' 1998 40cm high
'Pink Bucket' 1998 43cm high

left, background
Lawson Oyekan

33

Throughout the seventies the balance was maintained in a series of ceramic exhibitions which moved between the sculptural frontline – handbuilt, dry and irregular – and solace-giving thrown pottery – round, glazed, rhythmic (in Oliver Watson's terminology, *expressive* and *ethical* versions of the clay object). Mo Jupp, Gordon Baldwin, Graham Burr, Gillian Lowndes and Paul Astbury all belonged to the former category, and Janet Leach, Alan Caiger-Smith and David Leach to the latter. But side-stepping this division, in 1976 a major exhibition of work by Elizabeth Fritsch, *From Earth to Air*, further mapped out the territory for a New Ceramics dominated by pots rather than sculpture. But these were pots of an unfamiliar kind whose specialness was articulated by Peter Dormer in catalogue essays and in his 1986 book *The New Ceramics: Trends & Traditions*.

The 1980s was a confident and exciting decade for the British Crafts Centre, during which time the name was changed with a flourish to Contemporary Applied Arts. Sequences of significant exhibitions took place. Fliers to invite you to them became leaflets which one might keep (and in my case, one might write). It was a period which firmed up the professionalism of the crafts world. The market bloomed, international connections sprouted, working in ceramics seemed both more serious and more fun.

left
Lawson Oyekan
Red pot 1996
58cm high
White pot 1996
44cm high
'Manifestation of Dance' 1977
15cm high

below
Jacqueline Poncelet
'Give and Take' 1986
57cm long x 29 cm wide x 30cm high

Richard Slee
'Liar Liar, House on Fire' 1996
40cm high
'Stile' 1997
48cm high

right
Gillian Lowndes
'Can Collage' 1998
Porcelain dipped fibreglass, found objects
22cm high

The balance of expression and ethics continued – in 1984 Richard Slee and Richard Batterham both had exhibitions, in 1985 both Svend Bayer and Martin Smith, in 1986 Ewen Henderson and Janet Leach. At my own solo exhibition there in 1987, uniquely in my working lifetime, people queued up outside before it opened and only one piece was unsold at the end of the evening. In 1989 a group show entitled *Clay Bodies* was the first airing of a series of remarkable clay figures by Philip Eglin. There have been other moments of great impact, a sense of ceramic culture being shaped, in the long past of Contemporary Applied Arts. 1995 saw the retrospective show of Angus Suttie's work after his early death in 1993. The last pieces he made were elongated, flowing and intense.

In my exhibition *A View of Clay* for this celebratory year I tried to provide a long, if partial, view. Both William Newland, who has sadly died since the show, and Gordon Baldwin, taught me. Richard Slee and Jacqui Poncelet were my fellow students at the Central School and Royal College of Art in turn. I taught Philip Eglin and Lawson Oyekan at the College. Gwyn Hanssen Pigott and Clive Bowen I simply respect for the vital way they have taken bits of the Leach tradition and brought out something whole and distinct and fresh. I admire all of these artists, who have made up their own language with the material, and who show what a diverse and satisfyingly fictive world ceramics can be.

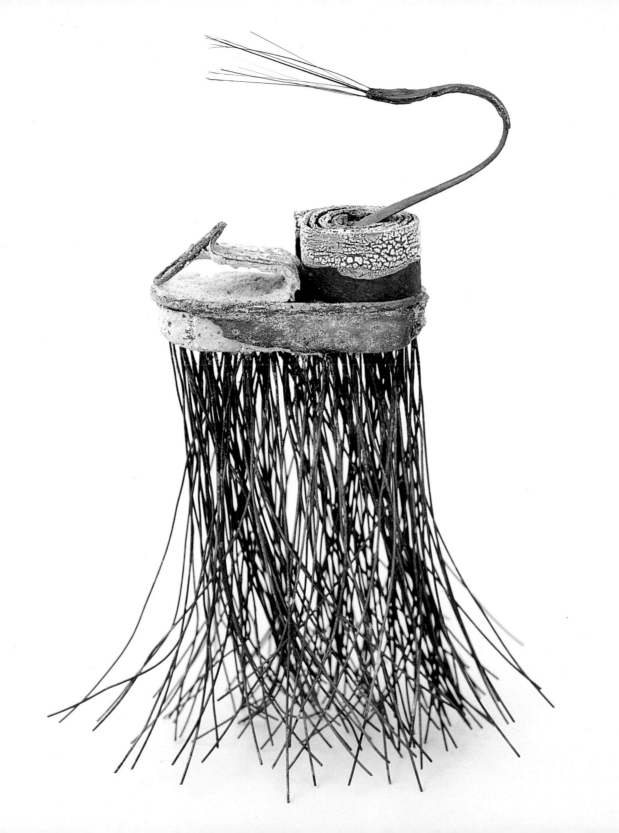

From the Diligent
to the Zany:
50 Years of Textiles on Show
Ann Sutton

Views of *Cloths of Gold* Exhibition 1998

Fifty years ago there were not many makers and very few opportunities for selling and exhibiting work: the Crafts Centre of Great Britain was there as a centre which never resorted to making ends meet by selling touristy items. Textiles then were mainly functional: rugs, table-mats, tweed lengths, block-printed cushions. This small double-fronted gallery was a haven for the growing number of discerning people whose needs were not yet met by Habitat. It complemented shops like Heals, Dunns of Bromley and the handful of like-minded furnishing retailers scattered across the country. Primavera in Sloane Street and Cambridge, was possibly the only other regular source of craft items.

There were the two exhibiting societies: the Red Rose Guild based in Manchester, and the Arts and Crafts Exhibition Society (renamed the Society of Designer-Craftsmen in 1959). Some regional Crafts Guilds (Devon and Hereford for instance) were happier when showing more traditional crafts. A few galleries emerged bravely: Peter Dingley in Stratford-upon-Avon among them. But the Crafts Centre was 'ours'. If accepted as members we could send in work which might be too experimental for the few shops in the field. The young could show, and sell, alongside the more experienced. And joy of joys, once the work was there we received a MONTHLY STATEMENT showing what was in stock, what had sold, and a cheque. This was achieved without the benefit of computers, of course. It was a lifesaver to craftsmen and craftswomen.

The Crafts Centre on Hay Hill was part shop, part gallery. Its weaver members included Gerd Hay-Edie, Peter Collingwood (who shared an exhibition with the potter Ruth Duckworth in 1964: he remembers selling a brushed mohair warp-faced rug), Tadek Beutlich, Barbara Sawyer, Ronald Grierson, Mary Barker, Jean Gytha, Gwen and Barbara Mullins, Theo Moorman, myself... There were almost certainly no knitters for knitting was not then a 'creative' form of textile making. (I remember as weave tutor in Worthing in the late 1950s, being chastised for 'allowing' students to knit in class; this was deemed akin to condoning smoking behind the bike-sheds). Embroiderer members included Constance Howard and Hebe Cox. Michael O'Connell's dramatic dye resist hangings were influential in encouraging interest in that technique and in the 1960s Noel Dyrenforth developed batik in a masterful fashion.

previous page
View of **Cloths of Gold** 1998
from left to right, all 30cm x 200cm
Kate Blee
'Organza Gold'
Painted silk organza layers
Dawn Dupree
'What Thrills You'
Pigment painted, discharge printed
double sided
Carole Waller
'Long Line'
Hand-dyed, screen printed silk organza layers
Sian Tucker
'Overlapping Circles'
Hand-painted double layer silk/organza
Sally Greaves-Lord
'Bee-Line'
Hand-painted, screen-printed silk
Michael Brennand-Wood
'The Golden Road To Unlimited Devotion'
Wood with inlaid fabric/metal structure
Natasha Kerr
'Refugee Kids'
Pigment-painted, silk-screen printed,
flocked antique cloth
Linda Miller
'Let Us Fly'
Machine embroidered shot-silk
Peter Collingwood
'Turband'
Folded, stitched 22m long Indian Turban

far left
Mary Restieaux
Ikat Weave 1998
Black, yellow,
white hand tie-dyed silk
30cm x 200cm

left
Sally Greaves-Lord
'Underground' 1998
Screen printed, handpainted
Silk panel 120cm x 240cm

41

The titles and themes of the early exhibitions at the Centre are suggestive in themselves. In 1952 there was an exhibition of Printed and Woven Textiles (including Tapestries, Lace and Embroidery), and in 1953, six weavers shared an exhibition with bookbinders. A 1954 exhibition of Furniture, Textiles and Pottery sounds like a classic combination of the period: 'Furniture to put the pots on, and textiles to hang behind the furniture or for the pots to stand on'. It was to be many years before textiles could shake off that 'background' role in exhibitions.

To complement the brown pots of the period, many of the textiles were also brownish. Printing took place on natural linen, as well as on slub silk in tasteful colours. Collingwood's rugs were breaking new ground technically, and so were Barbara Sawyer's table-mats. The table-mat was a new item in the textile maker's repertoire, and Barbara Sawyer realised it could be rolled, not folded, for storage. She started to space her warp out: creating closely set cotton stripes of up to one inch wide, with two-inch gaps between. Across this went a rigid weft: lengths of cane, rush and cellophane, interspersed with fancy cotton yarns. Tight knots, trimmed closely at the end of each mat, finished off a table-mat that became the ultimate accessory for the smart 1950s dining table, and the forerunner of every table-mat woven in India and the Philippines today.

The move to Earlham Street in 1966, with its larger wall spaces, coincided with the emergence of the big wall-hung textile, and was certainly instrumental in its development, showing the passing world how good these could look in the new larger living and corporate spaces. The late 1960s also saw a surge of interest in unique clothing marked at Earlham Street by a fashion show including dresses by Ossie Clark and work from the Royal College of Arts' School of Fashion. Exciting knitting, until then an oxymoron, was introduced by Kaffe Fassett and he was followed by many others, some of whom quickly graduated from personal production to the world of large quantities and export. Textiles vied with ceramics in terms of the sheer number of exhibitions. There were two or three textiles shows each year, many of them solo or two-person shows in which a philosophical, conceptual approach became the crucial element, not the material.

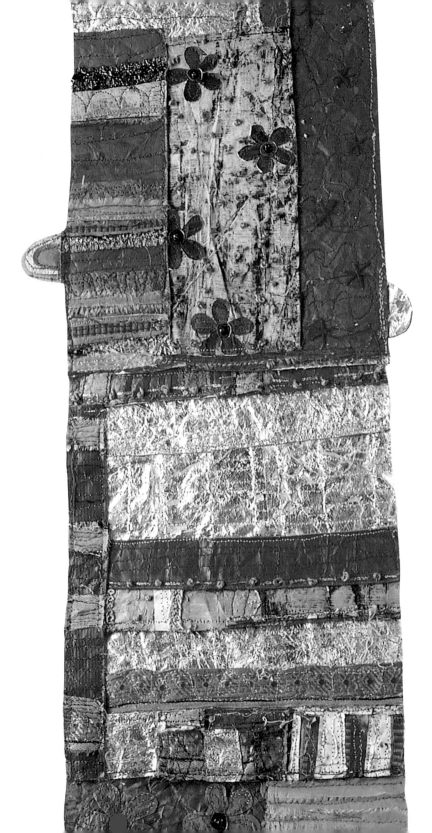

far left
Dawn Dupree
'What Thrills You' side one 1998
Pigment painted, discharge printed
double sided 30cm x 200cm

left
Dawn Dupree
'What Thrills You' side two 1998

right
Louise Baldwin
'Dark Track' (detail) 1998
Embroidered paper, fabric, gold leaf
beads, metal thread
30cm x 200cm

opposite from left to right
View of **Cloths of Gold** 1998
all 30cm x 200cm

Natasha Kerr
'Refugee Kids' (as before)

Neil Bottle
'Architectural Tapestry'
Hand-painted silk screen printed silk dupion

Louise Baldwin
'Dark Track' (see detail p43)

Nicola Henley
'Oystercatchers Feed on Gold'
Hand-dyed, painted, embroidered cotton

Sharon Ting
'Rainbow Filigree'
Hand-printed, sprayed silk organza
gathered with drawn threadwork

Archie Brennan
'Dear Penelope' (detail) 1998
Wool tapestry weave
30cm x 200cm

It was a happy time for exhibitors: I can remember the gratitude I felt when, after explaining how excited I was with the results of what I hoped was some fresh thinking in constructed textiles, I was immediately invited to have an exhibition of the knitted, woven, knotted, stitched, fluorescent plastic-y results. That exhibition in 1969 led directly to a small touring exhibition of textile image prints on paper and aluminium at the Victoria and Albert Museum: another example of the valuable springboard function of the Crafts Centre. Subsequent ventures such as *The House in the Yard*, an early stage of the textile collaboration of Roger Oates and Fay Morgan, were given a first airing in 1977 before hitting the mainstream world. The strong woven tapestry movement in Scotland was reflected in several exhibitions, dominated by the work of Archie Brennan, Fiona Mathison and Maureen Hodge. Peter Collingwood's cool macrogauzes were revealed to the public in the lofty space of the exhibition gallery.

The series of *International Exhibitions of Miniature Textiles*, the first held in 1974, introduced visitors to the idea of small pieces of textile, often with a strong conceptual content. And the prices of pieces sent in from other parts of the world introduced British textile artists to the idea that size and price were not necessarily related. Seeing my face at the price ticket of £2500 on a tiny American exhibit, Archie Brennan sagely remarked: 'Well, Ann, sometimes its better not to have sold something for £2500 than not to have sold it for £25'. By the end of the 1970s groups of 'fibre artists' began to flourish as textile makers fled from function in droves and attempted to join the art world. Goldsmiths' College was, however, the only art school to teach Art Textiles in a committed Fine Art way, and only a few of their graduates were drawn to Earlham Street.

Looking to the future, Contemporary Applied Arts's relocation to Percy Street heralds a new age of sophistication in textiles. My exhibition *Cloths of Gold* was one of the celebratory shows during its 50th year. It is one of only a handful in the history of Contemporary Applied Arts where makers have had restrictions placed upon them. As curator I asked my exhibitors to make a special piece for this special show in the form of a strip, up to 30cm wide and measuring 2m long. And it had to include the colour gold. The techniques included knitting, stitching, weaving, dyeing, printing, braiding... and some inventions. The guidelines proved to be popular. The results formed a forest of golden scarves, hangings, banners, runners. We invited many current members, of course, and a handful of non-members, a few of whom were members in those early days of Hay Hill. These included Peter Collingwood, Noel Dyrenforth, Tadek Beutlich, myself – and the request to 'Wear Gold!' provided a glittering and crowded opening. Zandra Rhodes' slinky gold dress, setting off her long shocking-pink hair as she opened the exhibition, and the tapestry weaver Candace Bahouth wearing a quilted gold sofa-shaped tissue box as a hat, showed that the current Contemporary Applied Arts continues to reflect all aspects of the textile arts, from the diligent to the zany.

right
Audrey Walker
'Caryatid' detail 1998
Embroidered silk
with darned gold thread.
Carved, painted wood heading
30cm x 200cm

left
Kumi Middleton
'Firebird' detail 1998
Knitted monofilament with silk,
copper wire, paper,
devoré wool, feathers, resin
30cm x 200cm

Golden Glory: Jewellery from Hay Hill to Percy Street

Graham Hughes

Wendy Ramshaw
Earrings 1998
18ct gold
12cm long

A fiftieth birthday is the perfect moment to look back and extract lessons from past experience, then to look forward and guess where those lessons are leading. I used to go to the committee meetings of the Crafts Centre of Great Britain, then our proud new crafts co-operative founded in 1948 by John Farleigh the wood engraver, and very boring they were. I remember Philip James, head of the new Arts Council, and champion of modern art, lamenting to me occasionally after meetings in our showrooms in Hay Hill, Mayfair, that the work on display was so uninteresting.

Among the thorny questions that were never resolved was how to evaluate our exhibits - must they be entirely made by hand, or would we allow, for instance, silver to be polished with a machine-driven wheel instead of being hand-burnished with an agate? Second, who should select exhibits – was a bookbinder, for instance, to be empowered to scrutinise silver, or must he or she have authority only over bookbindings? Third, how important were sales? We were always short of cash: there was no regular government subsidy, and even when the government grant was forthcoming, it was only a pathetic few hundred pounds. So our income came from meagre subscriptions, and from sales of exhibits. But sales were considered by some members to be ignoble. If once we became dependent on sales, the argument ran, we would soon become a depot for tourist trash. Most thorny of all, was the delegation of executive authority: should one person be allowed to run the place, or must everything be decided by the large committee which met on Saturday mornings, sometimes overrunning into the afternoon or evening.

I was chairman from 1965 until 1973. In April 1967 at the opening of the new Centre in Earlham Street, our architect Alan Irvine said to me, somewhat bewildered, 'Everyone's here'. It was true: a dazzling party of art pundits and collectors got us off to a great start. But our exhibits were a different story: the pots were lovely, though I remember an early director of ours, Michael Reeves, lamenting that he was sick of dark brown. The furniture and textiles were good too, solid if not thrilling. We yearned for more colour and enterprise, in technique as well as design. The silver, interpreting a centuries-old tradition, was slowly adapting itself

above
Dorothy Hogg
'Bangle with 50 Rings' 1998
22ct gold
9cm diameter

left
Mah Rana
'Love is like a butterfly' (detail) 1998
Recycled second-hand wedding bands,
preserved butterflies
Installation of 15 rings, 1m square

We had the odd film star visitor. On one amazing day when we were closed between exhibitions a man appeared knocking at the door. He was a rough looking fellow and I said 'We're closed' and he replied 'Oh, I've come all the way from Hollywood to see you' and I realised it was Rod Steiger, who was big in those days. He discovered that we were moving great chests of drawers and harpsichords about and he said 'Do you mean to say you do this – you don't have chaps to help you?' And he rolled up his sleeves and spent the morning moving things – he was a very good fellow.

Sheila Pocock

to market changes, acknowledging the importance of fashion. Silver had been well taught for decades at several art schools, especially the Central School of Art and Design and the Royal College of Art in London, with good teaching at Birmingham, Sheffield, Glasgow and Edinburgh. Small pieces by brilliant newcomers like Gerald Benney showed the way towards a renewal of the old skills of the hammerman. But jewellery was still in limbo. There were skilled workshops with apprentices, making big stone pieces for the Bond Street shops, but in art jewels there was really no equivalent yet to the 'Kitchen Sink' or 'Pop Art' schools of young painters.

A turning point was the *International Exhibition of Modern Jewellery* which I had organised at Goldsmiths' Hall in 1961. It showed how you can mix iron with diamonds, how jewels by Picasso, Braque or Dali were closer to abstract paintings than they were to the normal flower spray brooch. This was the first time that work in precious metals by great and famous creators had been gathered together, and its effect on artists and in the art world was electric. More and more art schools, like Loughborough, Canterbury or Aberdeen began to realise the potential of jewellery as an art form, at once liberating to the imagination, and at the same time implying a necessary and useful manual discipline. Brave pioneers like Gerda Flockinger from the Central School developed her personal style of enamels and abstract ornament which shocked some of the older practitioners. We gave her a big show at the Crafts Centre in 1968, her rectangular plaques suspended right across the ceiling. They were cheerful and spectacular, two characteristics which we have come to expect from our jewels today. But Gerda was almost unique. Another adventurer was Wendy Ramshaw with her lathe-turned ring clusters, as bright and precise as Gerda's were opaque and mystical.

Some of the Crafts Centre's function as public ambassador for skilled crafts was taken over by the Crafts Advisory Committee set up in 1971. The Centre then adopted a new name, the British Crafts Centre, and I left as chairman, and with me several of my craftsmen friends. Our declared aim had been to buy the cheap and splendid freehold of 43 Earlham Street, the best warehouse in Covent Garden, with crafts

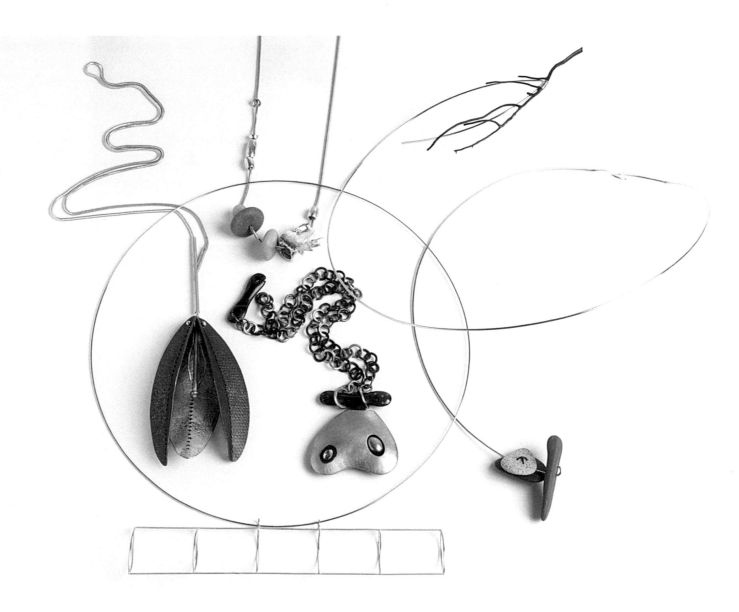

from left to right
Group of Necklaces, all made in 1998

Jane Adam
18ct gold leaf, sterling silver, aluminium

Holly Belsher
18ct gold, sterling silver, natural pebbles

Catherine Hills
18ct gold, oxidised sterling silver

Louise Slater
18ct gold, Cornish pebbles

main circle
Anna Gordon
18ct gold, steel

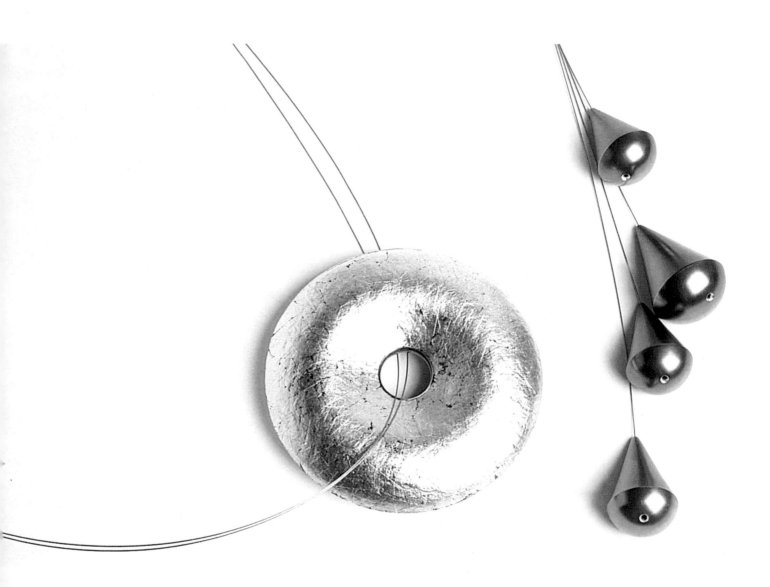

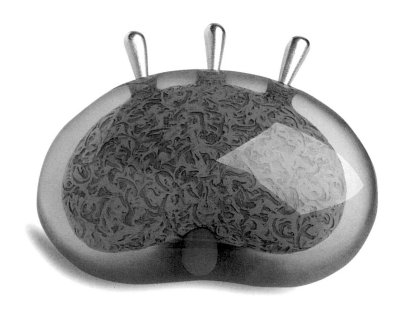

left
Maria Hanson
Neckpiece 1998
Gold-leafed limewood
10cm diameter
oxidised sterling silver, steel cable
160cm long

right
Dawn Gulyas
Brooch 1998
18ct gold, balsa wood, resin
8cm wide

workshops around it, thus forming a truly national centre for crafts. That this plan did not receive the support of the Crafts Advisory Committee now seems tragic. So we reach today, and what an encouraging scene it is! As fine art becomes increasingly self-centred and distances itself from the general public, so the crafts and especially jewellery, become ever more accessible.

Jewels have several advantages over the other crafts. You can make them at home because they do not need elaborate equipment nor large work spaces. The vocabulary of ornament is fresh and new, unlike for example teapots which have been manufactured for centuries and whose shapes have therefore become familiar. If you like the crafts – and many of us do because the machine has let us down in so many ways – then you can probably afford an art jewel, even if craft furniture, or ceramics by a named designer, may be beyond your means. Young jewellers today

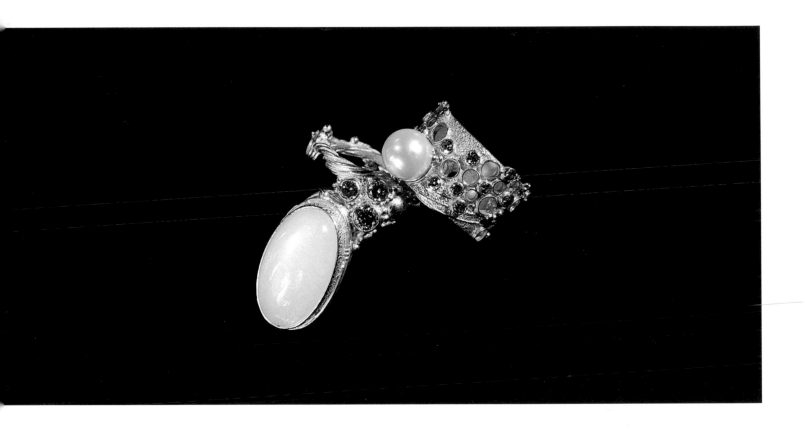

above
Gerda Flockinger
Pair of Rings 1993
18ct gold with long oval moonstone
and three brown diamonds
18ct gold with small dark diamonds and
cultured pearl

right
David Watkins
Brooch 1998 18ct gold
10cm diameter

work in all sorts of materials from paper, leather and wood to metals like titanium or even steel. There are now dozens of jewellery workshops in the bigger cities, in place of the one or two of fifty years ago, and Contemporary Applied Arts is well equipped to introduce you to them.

Not for decades has a British craft society been able to make decisions so firmly and quickly. Not for years has such good modern crafts presentation been possible in London, and the confident style there has earned its corollary, steadily increasing sales. Smaller but stronger must be the verdict after the first half century.

Hot Glass and Beyond
Jennifer Hawkins Opie

Sam Herman
Large Bottle Jar 1974
Blown glass with opaque colours, lustre surface
28cm high

right
Rachael Woodman
'Outcast' 1998
Free blown glass, cold finished
62cm high

below
Galia Amsel
'Dusk' 1998
Cast glass, palladium patina
65cm long

Studio glass has a short history. While Contemporary Applied Arts celebrates its fiftieth birthday, British studio glass is barely thirty. It is the most recent entrant into that crowded, competitive world, outside the factory system, and encompassing any work made by a designer using hand skills.

In January 1969 the Crafts Centre of Great Britain held its first solo hot glass exhibition. It was entirely devoted to the work of Sam Herman, the American glass-blower who was the catalyst for the launch of studio glass-making in Britain and it was a remarkable success. Herman had arrived only four years earlier and after a short spell in Edinburgh he was quickly enticed down to London, to the Royal College of Art as a Research Fellow.

Although art school training in glass at Stourbridge College of Art, closely followed by the Royal College of Art in London and the Edinburgh College of Art, had been well-established in Britain since the 1930s, this was entirely directed towards industry. Students were taught the skills necessary for the design of the object and its ornament. Engraving was the senior technique, hallowed by tradition and it provided the best (the only) opportunity for self-expression and first-hand engagement with the material. At Stourbridge students learned to work with the skilled glass-blower at the furnace, developing an understanding of form. After leaving art school they hoped to join an enlightened glass company which would expect them to design table and decorative wares for mass-production and, with luck, to be responsible for a more exclusively-marketed line of art-wares – and in the 1950s this was indeed possible for a few.

But Herman's arrival in Britain in 1965, quickly followed by an awareness of similar developments in Europe, changed everything. Hot glass-working became the hot subject and within a few years students had become professional glass-makers and had progressed well beyond the ill-formed bubble to an articulate glass vocabulary and ideas that were intellectual as well as technical. Peter Layton, Karlin Rushbrook, Ray Flavell and others pushed the frontiers forward.

right
Bob Crooks
'Metropolis Bowl' 1998
Free blown cased glass, cut and assembled
43cm x 39cm

below
Tessa Clegg
'Arco III & Arco II' 1998
Cast glass
31cm x 18cm & 24cm x 18cm

At this juncture an opportunity in Britain was lost. Had the British glass industry moved smoothly on from employing designer-engravers to using the imaginative ideas of hot glass designer-makers, the new craft skills would have become part of the mass-production vocabulary, and part of our everyday lives. Instead craft glass skills gradually became the province of the more exclusive world of collectors. The new makers, independent, owing nothing to industry, were free to make their own way.

Debate has flourished, even raged, ever since. Partly because of the mundane yet essential issue of selling in the first instance, and thereafter

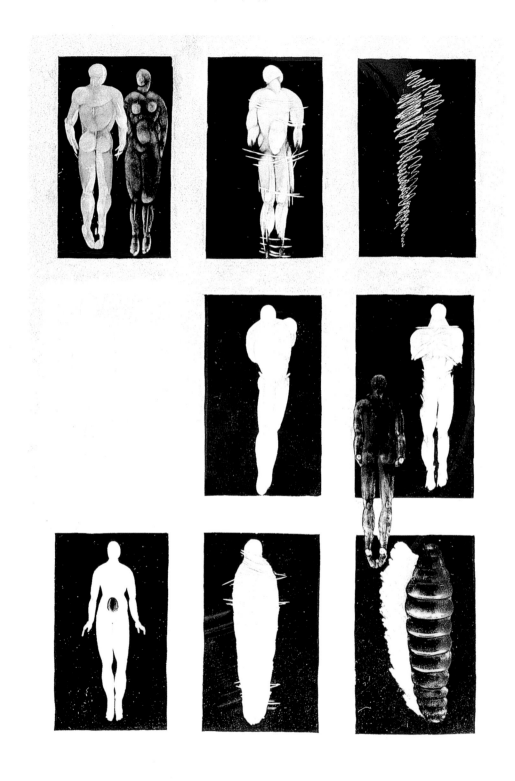

of price, makers have often found themselves caught between the bread and butter batch production of small items – drinking glasses, candlesticks and so on – and the ambition to express their individuality and explore technical possibilities; a lifelong studentship. The great idea, the artistic endeavour, the unique work was the prize – and this could also command a unique price. This division was translated into glass art versus mere functional craft – a damaging division and one which still operates today. And the old arguments about the improvement of the daily experience through 'well-designed', let alone artistically superior, mass-production have been swept off the table altogether.

Opportunities to present the new studio work to the public were – as now – limited and the Crafts Centre was one of the very few places to provide a regular showplace. Of equal importance, though even more limited, was the chance for the buying public to see hot glass being worked – a means of learning, understanding, an encouragement to purchase. In 1969, following Herman's exhibition, the Glasshouse was set up in Neal Street, next door to the Centre under the directorship of Graham Hughes, then the Centre's chairman, the Centre's director Susannah Robins and Herman. Thus the Crafts Centre provided the first opportunity for the public to walk off the street and watch hot glass-blowing. Since then the technique has been practised with masterly skill and aesthetic judgement by makers in all parts of the country; Simon Moore in London, Pauline Solven on the Welsh borders, Ray Flavell in Scotland.

After the first years of anarchy and anti-history, makers began to take an interest in the ancient traditions of the craft and during the late 1960s and the 1970s, some glass practitioners looked beyond hot glass. Most influentially, Keith Cummings at Stourbridge began experimenting with and teaching kiln-formed glass techniques and since then cast glass has occupied an increasingly large proportion of the stage. Cummings' own students, especially Tessa Clegg and Colin Reid, can justifiably claim to have invented an entirely new language in the technique. Meanwhile Diana Hobson pioneered a revival in Britain of the French technique of *pâte-de-verre*. David Reekie specialised in lost wax casting for his often complex compositions.

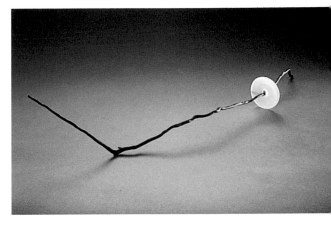

above
Diana Hobson
'Sea Root' 1996
Bronze and cast glass
59cm long

left
Alison Kinnaird
'Sampler I' (detail) 1997
Lead crystal, copper wheel engraved
30cm x 23cm

I was part of the team from 1970 to 1977, a fairly critical time in the history of the Centre in that it saw the birth of the Crafts Council and a fairly drastic change in policy. At first the budget was almost non-existent, and I clearly remember driving down to Devon or Dorset in my own car to collect pots to show in the Gallery; it simply would not have entered one's thinking to expect remuneration for this. There was, I suppose, a relaxed and enjoyable quality in the way we functioned, but it was not very 'professional' by today's standards.

Fiona Adamczewski

In a fiftieth anniversary celebration therefore, those glass makers chosen for the exhibition I curated demonstrate the journey of discovery, invention and creation that has led to studio glass now. Tessa Clegg has recently made a major change in her work, moving from an exploration of the bowl form to more abstract work, nonetheless retaining her powerful sense of form and absolute integrity. The engraver Alison Kinnaird displays, as always, imagination and formidable skill. Rachael Woodman, designer and glass-maker, has also made a significant break with her past in deconstructing her trademark 'bevelled bowls' and developing an entirely new palette. Sara McDonald works in laminated glass achieving a subtle three-dimensionality and Galia Amsel, working in cast glass, has a sense of landscape, exploring direction and interception. Bob Crooks is the hot glass-maker whose strengths, appropriately, are in a rapid turnover of ideas, creating glass which is immediate, glittering and attention-seeking.

British studio glass and its makers have many strengths. British glass, sometimes seen as understated, none the less has developed an expressive and flexible language in which its makers have increasing confidence. Multi-media and a mix of techniques have become increasingly the norm. Metals, wood and stone are all used to provide context for glass. British makers draw important strengths from contacts abroad. Ray Flavell trained in Sweden. Elizabeth Swinburne in the Netherlands. Clare Henshaw has worked in Australia and several glass-makers have spent time in the Czech Republic. Diana Hobson now works partly in America. Still others have settled abroad. Clifford Rainey and Arlon Bayliss live and work in America, Stephen Proctor and Jane Bruce in Australia. In reverse, Göran Wärff, Steven Newell, Bibi Smit, Keiko Mukaide, Danny Lane and Lisa Autogena have all spent time in Britain or settled here. Tessa Clegg, David Reekie and Anna Dickinson sell their work almost exclusively to Japan, Europe and America. As this international exchange is developed and British art glass becomes part of the global glass fraternity, creative glass clearly has not only a secure future but also a healthy one.

Sara McDonald
'Bowl with Grid/Maze'
Fused with inclusions and slumped
60cm diameter

Solace and Renewal: The Real Life of Pots
Edmund de Waal

Julian Stair
Triangular red stoneware Caddy 1998
15cm high

'Proofs weary the truth.' Braque

There has always been much weary business around the making of functional pots in England. There have been manifestos of different degrees of passion (*Towards a Standard, Quo Vadis?*), the claiming of high grounds, the ceding of territory, skirmishes about self-definition and values, the foundation of magazines and associations, committees and resignations, the writing of partial histories. Think of the long trajectory of names adopted: potter, artist-craftsman, ceramicist, ceramist, maker, artist-in-clay; the wearisome impression is of a world turned in on itself, of familial generations distancing themselves from each other. Sometimes it appears close to the condition of accidie, the listless paralysis that came on monks too long in their cells, over-habituated to their cloistered life. And the positions taken have often been dogmatic, oppositional, doctrinaire and self-consciously counter-cultural. Think, for example, of Standard Ware, the attempt to make everything that a household could need in Orientalist stoneware. There is no getting away from the fact that pottery this century, and in particular this half-century since the creation of the Crafts Centre of Great Britain and its inheritor Contemporary Applied Arts, has been an anxious art, and that its anxiety has often made it strident, even cross. Think of Michael Cardew's fierce question, at the nadir for respect of domestic pottery in the 1980s, '. . . are you a potter? Answer yes or no.'

Why is pottery anxious about itself? Firstly because it is an art that is profoundly demotic in its reach. Any art that can accommodate so many different kinds of facture, so many different kinds of things, trembles on the edge of dissolution. Can the centre hold when an art seems so readily understandable? Can it be taken seriously when it can be so cheap? An art needs its arcanum, its mysteries and its acolytes to translate its secrets to be a proper art. The mug, casual metonym for pottery, holds few secrets so it becomes a mere bagatelle in the worlds of material culture-shopping and decorating. Bernard Leach was a good barometer of this fear of dissolution. In the late 1920s he showed his 'art pots' in one London gallery and his 'domestic pots' in another gallery at the same time. The critics wrote of his fortune at finding a 'suitable place of banishment' for the domestic: two kinds of pottery made by one

left
Walter Keeler
Jug 1998
creamware,
polychrome decoration,
crabstock handle
16cm high

below
Joanna Constantinidis
Porcelain Cup and Saucer 1998
10.5cm diameter

right
Takeshi Yasuda
Milk Jugs
creamware
14cm high, 10cm high

below
Walter Keeler
1998
Jug green tigerskin 15cm high
Jug green tortoiseshell 13cm high
Teapot gold and green 19cm high

potter was a diminishment of accomplishment. It induced anxiety. In the late 1930s Leach showed his pots at the Little Gallery alongside Edward Bawden wallpaper, artefacts from Sweden and India and Wedgwood china. A confident expression of pottery as an art-form? A secure placement of pots as part of contemporary material culture? Or a good place to sell? The reality is that whether shown alongside avant-garde paintings (as William Staite Murray did for a short time in the early 1930s) or shown as part of a decorating *mise-en-scene* (Leach at the Little Gallery, Lucie Rie in Heals in the 1950s) pots have rarely animated a gallery-space in the lonely way that it is understood that art should. They have been shown with other *things*. And this has been a powerful animus in the feeling that pots are still looking for a home.

left
Rupert Spira
(foreground)
1998
Takeshi Yasuda
(background, left and centre)
1998
Julian Stair 1998
(background right)

right
Clive Bowen
Square dish 1997 *(on table)*
Green tall jug 1997
Green jug 1997
Large lidded jar 1997
Large black jar 1997
65cm high

Pottery has also been an anxious art because it has borrowed so many languages, critical, conceptual and metaphorical, to reinstate its particularity and specialness, that the air is thick with airs and graces. Of course every discipline needs a language, and a critical vocabulary, to make sense of itself. But there has often been a sense of philosophy and aesthetics being used for aggrandisement rather than explication. The result has been that the rich, strange heart of the subject – why pots have this ability to move, unsettle and console us – remains unexplored.

It may be of value to restate a few home-truths. They begin with the fact that pottery can be useful, that it occupies an actual and symbolic place within the domestic, close to the hearth. It is part of the day to day, the unregarded and the quotidian. As such it has the rare and extraordinary ability to be part of our intimate understanding of how we eat, drink

During the days at Hay Hill, I was on the committee of the Arts and Crafts Exhibition Society, which held its meetings in an upstairs room above the Crafts Centre. One evening our preoccupation was with the standards of craftsmanship we should expect from prospective members. 'We cannot accept potters who do not turn their bases', Victor Margrie pronounced, just as other members suggested rules of craftsmanship for their own disciplines. Notes were taken, and at nine o'clock we finished the meeting highly satisfied with our work. As we went down to the entrance, we passed through the exhibition of pots by Hamada. 'But Victor, we wouldn't accept him into our Society', I commented. We went back upstairs and cancelled the rules which had just been made.

Ann Sutton

During the mid fifties, Bernard Leach took me to task for contaminating clay by putting 'foreign matter' into it. He also said that the abstract birds I was using as knobs and handles reminded him of children's clockwork toys, although I don't remember heeding these strictures when Victor Margrie and I held our joint 1962 exhibition at the Crafts Centre at Hay Hill. Here Bernard claimed to need a helping hand to lift one of my jugs, and, in the manner of Edith Evans when told that a rather flamboyant pot I had made was for bread, expostulated, 'Bread! Surely not, you must mean cakes!'

Michael Casson

and offer food. But it is also on thresholds between different public and private worlds: it is a liminal artform. This is because a teapot or beaker can move between kitchen shelves and draining-board and a mantelpiece, vitrine or museum: this potentiality is a key strength of the real life of pots. It is also a strength that can be explored by potters concerned to interrogate the ways in which traditions of pottery are reinvigorated: to show how the old can reignite the contemporary. A kitchen cupboard can contain real conversations across cultures.

Another home truth is that pots are an extraordinary and intense focus, a nexus, of the visual and the performative. That is to say they exist as objects with visual meanings of tonality and colour, form and profile, and with the somatic meanings that can occur only when they are picked up and handled. They can have powerful haptic resonances too; our bodily range of memories of touch and balance are far deeper than is often thought. That these memories are not just contemplative but can be abrasive and challenging is an important point: pots are not just objects for solace. And then pottery is also a performative art: a pot 'comes alive' experientially through handling.

If pottery can have so many levels of meaning, why is it not taken more seriously? Whereas the plaudits over the last generation have gone almost exclusively to a group of ceramicists who have told of their interest in the fictional and metaphorical possibilities of domestic sculpture, vessels and ceramic sculpture, there has been a resultant great lacuna in thinking about pots. Pointing out just how innovative pots can be, how interrogative of traditions, how capable they are of being both things for solace and things for renewal, objects for the centres of our lives as well as the liminal, is long overdue. There is no need for anxiety.

It is a good time to be a potter, to be making pots.

Edmund de Waal
Large Lidded Jars
1998
Porcelain, celadon glaze
38cm high

Ceramics through Time
Elizabeth Fritsch

Elizabeth Fritsch
Green Horn Vase
'Collision of Particles' 1995
16cm high

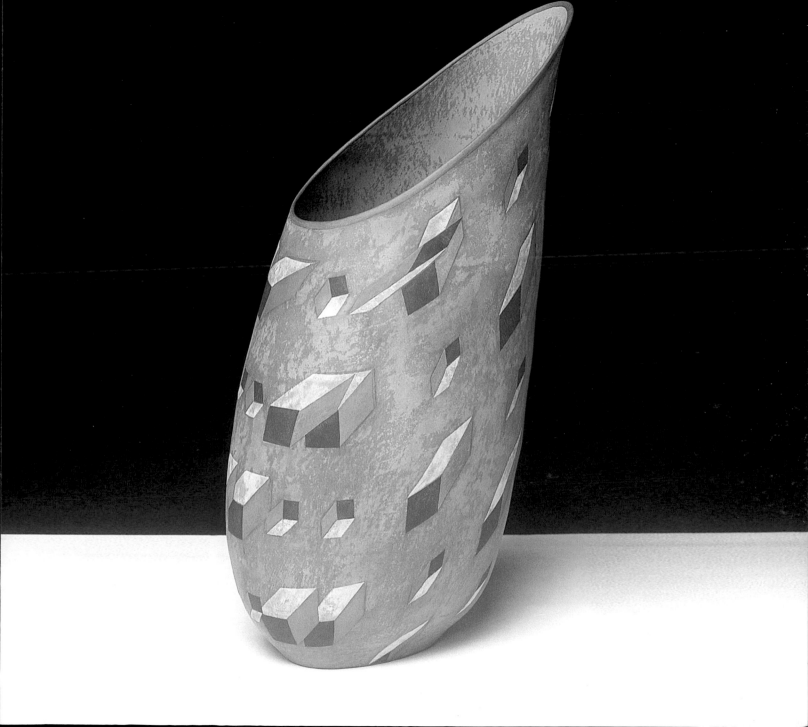

This was written by Elizabeth Fritsch in 1976 for the invitation card to her British Crafts Centre exhibition Improvisations from Earth to Air. *Swiftly penned in note form, it reads like a precise, powerful manifesto.*

left
Elizabeth Fritsch
Blown Away Vase
'Collision of Particles' 1996
57cm high

Lachrymatory for the Death
of a Poet
'Collision of Particles' 1996
41cm high

Improvisations from Earth to Air

Liz Fritsch (pots) and Veryan Weston (piano) collaborating on the basis of their common ground/air.

Each piece of music and pottery shares in being:

1. unrepeatable – ie improvised.
2. hand-made and unmechanistic.
3. intimate in scale and accessible (e.g. pots to be held).
4. minimal in resources – i.e. two hands plus craft.
5. rooted in the love of ethnic music and craftsmanship – i.e. work should be a joy in itself but also have a useful function.
6. eclectic and influenced by 20th century (e.g. in the frequent use of fragmentation).
7. structured using such devices as counter-point, polyrhythms, cross rhythms, arpeggios, modulations, sequences, etc.
8. technically prepared – i.e. aspiring towards dynamic precision.
9. inspired by elemental cross-currents e.g. two earth-bound pots aspire to become airborne (musical) in their forms, colours, geometric articulations and in their inter-relationships in groups.
10. made primarily for love (as opposed to money) – the pots try to emulate the insubstantiality of music and to transcend commodity status – hence this collaboration.

right
Elizabeth Fritsch
'Night Waves'
Large 42cm high
Small 29cm high

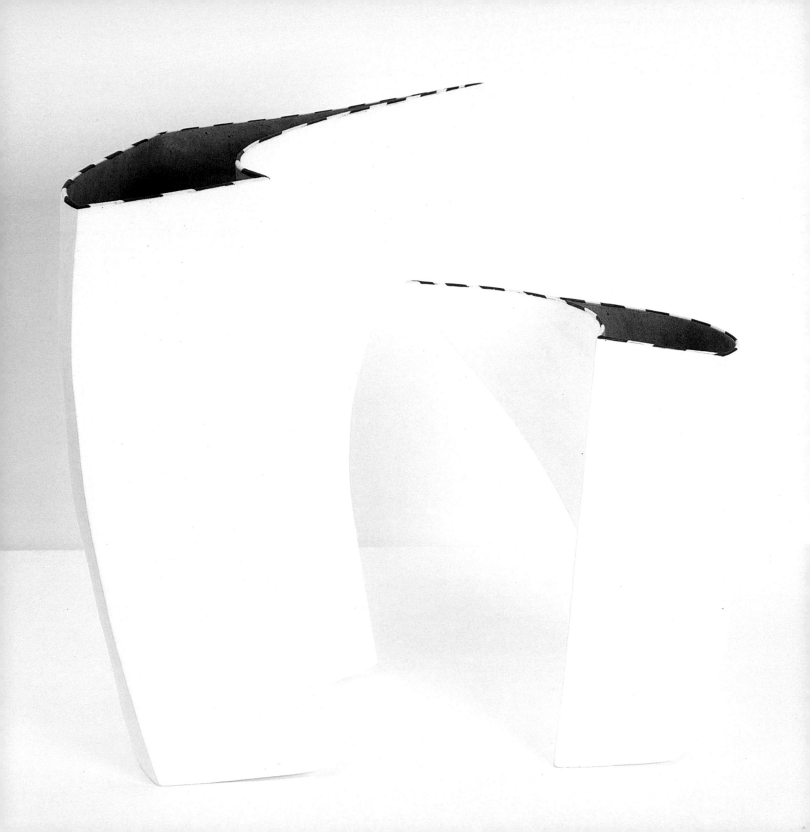

Appendix

compiled by Adrian Bland

Nomenclature over Fifty Years
Crafts Centre of Great Britain 1948-1972
British Crafts Centre 1972-1986
Contemporary Applied Arts 1987-

Directors and General Secretaries
Trevor Thomas 1947-1948
Evelyn Fahy (General Secretary) 1946-1954
Sheila Pocock (General Secretary) 1954-1964
Margaret Davenport (General Secretary) 1964-1965
Cyril Wood 1964
Lloyd Fraser 1965-1969
Susannah Robins 1969-1974
Victor Margrie (temporary Director) 1972-1973
Michael Sellers 1974-1977
Caroline Pearce-Higgins (acting Director) 1977-1978
Malcolm MacIntyre-Read 1978-1980
Karen Elder 1980-1983
Tatjana Marsden 1983-1990
Tessa Peters 1990-1994
Mary La Trobe-Bateman 1994-

Chairpersons
John Farleigh 1946-1964
David Kindersley 1964-1965
Reginald Marlow 1965-1966
Graham Hughes 1966-1973
Nigel Vinson (joint chair) 1972
Sir Duncan Oppenheim (acting chair) 1973
Alan Caiger-Smith 1974-1977
Archie Brennan and Mervyn Ungar 1977-1978
Faith Shannon (acting chair) 1978
Lindsay Wilcox 1979-1994
Martin Smith (acting chair) 1994-1996
Nicholas Mann 1996-

Acknowledgements

The Editors would like to thank all the contributors to this volume and all those who responded to requests for information, in particular two former General Secretaries of the Crafts Centre, Sheila Pocock and Tarby Davenport. Adrian Bland proved an able assistant, encouraging a range of makers and others connected with the Centre/CAA to put their memories down on paper. Both he and Sonia Collins worked hard on a comprehensive list of exhibitions, which will be published later.

Telos would like to thank David Eno and Paul Richardson

CONTEMPORARY APPLIED ARTS

HAND
TO
HAND